# Debbie Shore's SEWING JOURNAL

Your personal reference guide to designing, planning and sewing your own projects

50 SEARCH PRESS

This journal belongs to:

................................................................

................................................................

If found, please contact:

................................................................

................................................................

# Contents

## Starting out ..... 4
Introduction ..... 4
How to use your journal ..... 5
About me ..... 6
Setting your intentions ..... 8
Body measurements ..... 10

## Sewing essentials ..... 16
All about fabrics ..... 17
Your tool kit ..... 40
Colour ..... 52

## Project planning ..... 58
Getting organized ..... 59
Project planners ..... 62
Monthly planners ..... 142

## Sewing reference ..... 156
Mending ..... 157
Quilting ..... 163
Dressmaking ..... 168
Homewares ..... 176
Sewing glossary ..... 180

## Final thoughts ..... 182

# STARTING OUT

## Introduction

Welcome to your sewing journal! I've partially filled the book with ideas, hints and tips, useful information and a few fun ditties. Your job is to fill the rest of the pages with your personal information and ideas, shopping and to-do lists – and together we'll create a personal go-to reference journal just for you!

*Debbie xo*

# How to use your journal

Use **about me** (page 6) to start recording your personal sewing journal. Add your own **body measurements**, and those of anyone else you sew for (pages 11–13). Not sure how to measure? Take a look at **how to take body measurements** (pages 174–175) for advice.

Add notes about your **sewing machine** (page 47) and reminders when it's due a clean! Write down your **stitch settings** (page 49) so you'll always have a note of the length and width you've used for a particular project. I find this helpful for satin stitching appliqué – I can never remember the best settings!

Make notes of the fabrics and notions you need to buy in the **project planners** (pages 62–141), then save a swatch of your favourite fabrics for your **fabric stash** (pages 30–35). Don't forget to make a note of where you bought them from and how much you paid for them!

Not sure what needle size to use? Take a look under **your tool kit** (pages 40–41) for a simple explanation. If you find sewing jargon confusing, there's a **glossary** at the end (page 180), and more terms are explained throughout the journal.

Note down important dates and plan your sewing projects over the seasons with the **monthly planners** to fill in (pages 142–155).

Add your own words of wisdom in your **notes to my future self** (page 183) – slip-ups you've made along your sewing journey, good advice that you've been given and things you've learned along the way. Mine says 'it always looks better second time around'; if I make a mistake and have to start again, the result is always better than the first.

There is plenty of space for your own personal notes throughout the journal, and even a page for you to put a picture of something that makes you happy to cheer you up on any days you find a struggle (page 7). I have a picture of my dog, Bobbin, on my page which always makes me smile!

Don't expect your journal to be neat and tidy! There should be scribblings, swatches, doodles and sketches as you plot your sewing journey.

# About me

Use this page to jot down some notes about yourself – this journal is about you after all! Perhaps why you love sewing or any personal information you might like to look back on in future.

## Things that make me happy...

STARTING OUT

**MY FAVOURITE**..........................

*Stick in a photo of something that makes you smile...*

**MY FAVOURITE**..........................

*...or perhaps a photo of a happy memory.*

# Setting your intentions

What are your sewing goals? Do you have unfinished projects or is there a new skill you'd like to learn?

Write down your goals opposite so you don't forget, then give yourself a well-deserved pat on the back when you've achieved each of them.

Remember, nobody was born an expert! We've all practised and failed before succeeding, and there will always be new things to learn.

Look back through this journal in twelve months' time and see how far you've come! Then save it, revisit it each year and compare your journals and journey over the years. You'll be amazed at what you've accomplished – well done from me to the future you!

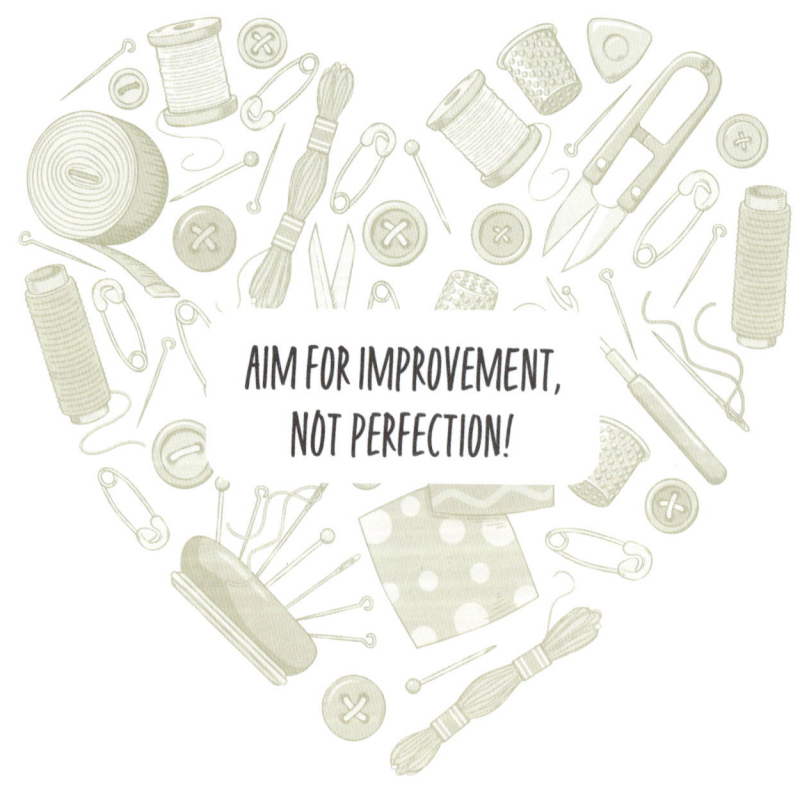

AIM FOR IMPROVEMENT, NOT PERFECTION!

# My intentions...

This year I would like to:

# Body measurements

Fill in your details so you don't have to measure each time you make a garment. Remember, no one's going to see this but you, so be honest!

You can also note down the measurements of people you regularly sew for, and then you will have them to hand when making special gifts.

See pages 174–175 for more on how to take body measurements.

## MY MEASUREMENTS

| Name: | | Date: | |
|---|---|---|---|
| Bust/Chest: | | Neck: | |
| Waist: | | Shoulder to shoulder: | |
| Hips: | | Shoulder to wrist: | |
| Waist to knee: | | Waist to floor: | |
| Inside leg: | | Other: | |
| Notes: | | | |

## FRIENDS AND FAMILY MEASUREMENTS

| Name: | | Date: | |
|---|---|---|---|
| Bust/Chest: | | Neck: | |
| Waist: | | Shoulder to shoulder: | |
| Hips: | | Shoulder to wrist: | |
| Waist to knee: | | Waist to floor: | |
| Inside leg: | | Other: | |
| Notes: | | | |

## Name:                                    Date:

| | |
|---|---|
| Bust/Chest: | Neck: |
| Waist: | Shoulder to shoulder: |
| Hips: | Shoulder to wrist: |
| Waist to knee: | Waist to floor: |
| Inside leg: | Other: |

Notes:

## Name:                                    Date:

| | |
|---|---|
| Bust/Chest: | Neck: |
| Waist: | Shoulder to shoulder: |
| Hips: | Shoulder to wrist: |
| Waist to knee: | Waist to floor: |
| Inside leg: | Other: |

Notes:

## Name:                                    Date:

| | |
|---|---|
| Bust/Chest: | Neck: |
| Waist: | Shoulder to shoulder: |
| Hips: | Shoulder to wrist: |
| Waist to knee: | Waist to floor: |
| Inside leg: | Other: |

Notes:

## STARTING OUT

**Name:**          **Date:**

| | |
|---|---|
| Bust/Chest: | Neck: |
| Waist: | Shoulder to shoulder: |
| Hips: | Shoulder to wrist: |
| Waist to knee: | Waist to floor: |
| Inside leg: | Other: |

Notes:

---

**Name:**          **Date:**

| | |
|---|---|
| Bust/Chest: | Neck: |
| Waist: | Shoulder to shoulder: |
| Hips: | Shoulder to wrist: |
| Waist to knee: | Waist to floor: |
| Inside leg: | Other: |

Notes:

---

**Name:**          **Date:**

| | |
|---|---|
| Bust/Chest: | Neck: |
| Waist: | Shoulder to shoulder: |
| Hips: | Shoulder to wrist: |
| Waist to knee: | Waist to floor: |
| Inside leg: | Other: |

Notes:

## EIGHT DAYS A WEEK

If I could make it happen,
If I could have my way,
I'd unpick Tuesday and Wednesday
And sew in an extra day.

I'd call the day 'Sewday'
If it was within my powers,
As I'd spend the day just sewing
For those extra twenty-four hours.

I'd make a bag, I'd make a quilt,
I'd probably make a mess!
I'd finish off my UFOs
And then I'd make a dress.

I wouldn't sleep, I wouldn't eat,
You know where this is going...
There's just no time for any of that
When the day is filled with sewing!

So when my day is finished
And I've made so much stuff,
I'd need to sew another day
One day is not enough!

## Notes...

# SEWING ESSENTIALS

This section of your journal covers some sewing basics that you can refer back to over again whenever you need to. We look at common fabric types, tools and their uses, choosing the right needle for the job, and how to care for your all-important sewing machine!

When you find fabrics and notions you like, use this section of your journal to make a note of why you liked them, where to buy them from and how much they cost, and if possible add a small swatch or sample to remind you.

We also take a look at choosing colour combinations, so you can find the perfect colour theme to suit you or your home décor!

# All about fabrics

When choosing fabrics, always read the instructions thoroughly and take guidance from the pattern designer – they have created the garment/bag/quilt with specific fabrics in mind. A visit to a local fabric store may be helpful if you're not sure what fabric is suitable for your project, and gives you a chance to feel the texture and weight to make sure you're happy with it.

## FABRIC TYPES

There are so many different types and blends of fabrics – natural and synthetic – that listing them would be a whole new book! In this section I'm just going to cover the ones I think you'll use most and what you'd use them for. On that note, there's no reason why you can't use a fabric for a project that may at first seem inappropriate. For instance, viscose or lawn aren't strong fabrics so you wouldn't normally use them for bags, but add a firm interfacing and they'll be strong enough. And if you really want to use that jersey but don't need the stretch, add a non-stretch interfacing on the back and use it anyway!

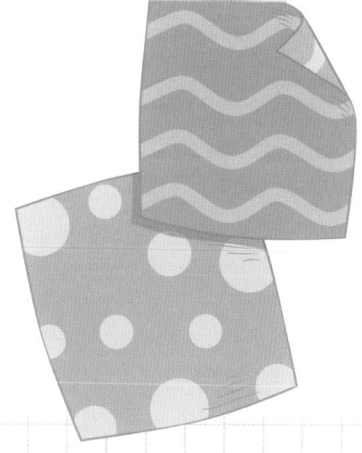

# COTTON FABRICS

Cotton is made from natural fibres and is simple to look after. It's the most commonly used fabric in the world, and comes in many weaves, weights and knits – many of which you might not think of as cotton! Here are some examples.

## CANVAS
Strong fabric that is used for home décor and outer garments, some are treated to be waterproof. Duck canvas is more tightly woven and has a higher thread count.

**Needle:** A denim or jeans needle would work well.

## LAWN
A fine fabric with a high thread count which gives it a smooth texture. Perfect for floaty dresses and blouses.

**Needle:** A universal needle, nothing special needed.

## POPLIN
Lightweight fabric with a tight weave, relatively crease-free. Perfect for dressmaking, bag linings and cushion covers. Poplin can also be made from viscose, wool and silk.

**Needle:** A universal needle will work well.

## CHAMBRAY
Fine fabric with coloured lengthwise threads, usually blue, and a white crosswise thread. It looks like a lightweight denim. Great for shirts, dresses and childrenswear.

**Needle:** Again, use a universal needle.

## CORDUROY
This can be fine or thick, baby or jumbo! The fabric has ridges known as wales which can vary in width. It is soft but durable, ideal for pinafores, jackets and homewares.

**Needle:** A strong denim or jeans needle is suitable for heavier fabrics.

## JERSEY

A soft, stretchy knit fabric that is easy to work with as it doesn't fray. The edges have a tendency to curl, so a generous dose of spray starch will help before cutting! Double knit like Ponte de Roma is created by knitting two layers of fabric together with multiple needles.

**Needle:** Use a jersey or ball point needle for best results. These have a rounded end so won't tear the threads as you stitch through them.

## DENIM

A sturdy textile which has diagonal ribbing, available in many colours but the most common is indigo blue.
**Needle:** Denim or jeans needle.

*I once visited my grandparents wearing jeans. My grandad said 'Why are you wearing overalls?' He was a steam engine driver and wore denim overalls to work, so he was quite shocked when this fabric became fashionable! It's not printable what he said about platform shoes...*

# OTHER FABRICS

Some other fabrics you might come across are polyester/poly mixes, viscose, laminates, crêpe and bouclé.

### POLYESTER/POLY MIXES

Made from man-made synthetic fibre, this material is durable, colourfast and doesn't shrink. Polyester blended with fabric such as cotton makes it breathable – and clever manufacturing these days makes it difficult to tell the difference! As a child, my dressmaker mum used a lot of crimplene as it didn't need ironing – I grew up in the 1960s surrounded by static!

**Needle:** Use a universal needle.

### CRÊPE

Made from many types of fibre, crêpe has a slightly crinkled surface created by twisted yarns.

**Needle:** A universal needle is fine.

### VISCOSE

A semi-synthetic fabric made from wood pulp. It has a fluid drape and makes fabulous floaty skirts and dresses.

**Needle:** A universal needle is fine.

*Back in the 1970s... I made a pair of hotpants from quite thick faux leather – so uncomfortable but I looked so fashionable!*

## LAMINATES

Laminated fabric is usually a cotton-based material with a PVC coating that makes it shiny and waterproof. It's quite easy to sew with – a non-stick foot will allow the fabric to glide under the needle without sticking. Be aware that a needle will make holes in the fabric, so if you want to re-waterproof it then use a little wet fabric glue over the holes. Iron on the reverse (from the cotton side), and always test a small piece first to make sure it will take the heat.

**Needle:** A universal 12 or 14 or denim needle will be fine.

## BOUCLÉ

This is a woollen fabric with loosely woven loops and curls over the surface. It is commonly used for jackets.

**Needle:** Use a universal needle. A walking foot will help the fabric travel smoothly through the machine.

## FELT

A non-woven fabric made from either natural or synthetic fibres, felt is a great fabric for craft items, toys and appliqué as it doesn't fray, and makes a perfect backdrop for hand sewing stitches with embroidery thread.
**Needle:** Use a universal needle.

## FLEECE

Knitted fabric with a pile, made from cotton blends or polyester, used for toys and leisure wear.
**Needle:** Use a jersey/ball point needle.

## CHIFFON

Luxurious, soft and sheer! As you can see through the fabric, use a French seam and avoid back-tacking as the seams and stitches on the inside will be seen. Leave the threads long enough to hand knot at each end. A rolled hem works best, use a short stitch.
**Needle:** Use a fine needle: 60/8 or 65/9.

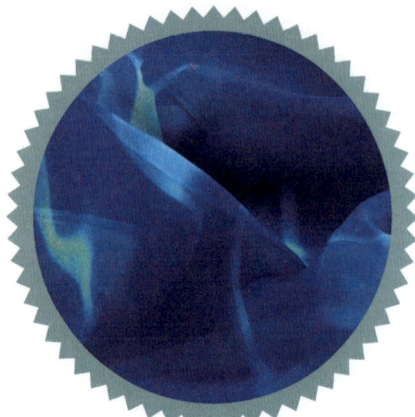

## VELVET AND VELOUR

Velvet (shown on the right) has a short, thick pile and a luxurious feel, made from silk, cotton or the more affordable rayon or polyester. Make classy throws, cushions, curtains and upholstery, jackets and even ballgowns!

Velour is the knitted version of velvet. The pile is not quite as long and doesn't have the shine that velvet has.
**Needle:** Use a universal 70/10 needle, a stretch needle for velour.

## GINGHAM

A woven fabric usually using two colours to create a checked pattern. You can trust a weave to be straight, but be careful with printed checks as the checks may not be completely straight!
**Needle:** Again, use a universal needle.

## WOOLLEN FABRICS

Wool fabrics come in many weights, heavy to light, knitted or woven, but be aware most of them will shrink! Pre-shrunk wool is available to buy, or just remember that the finished item will probably need to be dry cleaned.
**Needle:** Use a ball point needle.

## BLENDER

These are fabrics that have a little more interest in the print than just a plain, but not too bold as to overshadow your printed fabrics.
**Needle:** Usually quilting weight cotton, a universal needle is fine.

## SATIN

A slippery, shiny fabric used for lingerie, nightwear, bed sheets, blouses and linings. It's advisable to cut one layer at a time to prevent slippage. Cut the fabric in the same direction as the light may reflect differently in different directions. Water can stain satin, so avoid steam from the iron.
**Needle:** Use a fine needle. Microtex work well as they are very sharp.

# Interfacings and linings

Stabilizers, interfacing, wadding, batting, fleece... what's the difference? Let's keep it simple with the following...

**Stabilizer** provides structure to your fabric and is usually removed after sewing. Interfacing also adds structure but becomes part of the project. Stabilizer would be used when machine embroidering to prevent the fabric from stretching and puckering, or when machine sewing buttonholes for the same reason.

**Tear-away stabilizer** this is my choice for most projects. Some tear-aways have a sticky back or can be ironed on to your fabric.

**Wash-away stabilizer** is water-soluble, good when used on top of fabric with a pile such as towelling or fleece.

**Heat-removable stabilizer** dissolves with the heat from your iron.

**Cut-away stabilizer** is where the stabilizer is trimmed to the stitches after sewing, so a little of the fibre remains in the project.

**Interfacing** is usually used in collars, cuffs, waistbands, pockets and necklines to add firmness or prevent stretching. It can be **fusible** which is the easiest choice, but on a loose-weave fabric a sew-in interfacing would be more suitable as the glue on a fusible may come through the weave.

**Non-woven interfacing** has no grain so can be used in any direction, and is suitable for most projects.

With **woven interfacing** you'll need to match the grain line if you're using woven fabrics. It can also be used with knit fabrics such as jersey to prevent it from stretching.

**Knit interfacing** is also available, if you need to add structure to knitted fabric but want to keep the stretch. The weight of interfacing should generally be the same or lighter than the weight of the fabric. Test on a small piece of the fabric you're using to check how it feels and drapes before committing to the pattern pieces!

**Wadding/batting** (these are the same thing, depending on which country you're in! Let's just call it wadding for now...) This is the unsung hero of the sewing world, the fluffy bit that goes in between a quilt top and backing fabric (quilt sandwich). You may not see it in a finished project but don't scrimp – wadding can make a big difference to the look and feel of a quilt. There are many fibre choices, and my go-to for quilting is a blend of cotton and polyester, 80/20. It drapes well and is easy to care for.

There are many more types of wadding available that serve their own purposes, but these are my favourites for most of my projects.

I use **polyester wadding** for projects that need laundering regularly. As it is more cost effective, it works well for bags and wall hangings too.

**Bamboo** can be blended with cotton to make a luxurious eco-friendly option, and choose **silk wadding** if you're hand sewing as it is so soft and lightweight and has a beautiful drape. The 'loft' is the thickness of the wadding: high loft is lovely to quilt with as the stitches just sink into the fabric, while low loft gives a flatter finish.

**Fleece** is typically a non-woven polyester that can be fusible or sew-in, and comes in a choice of thicknesses. I regularly use fusible for bags of all sizes both to give structure and prevent any stretch in the fabric. I use Vlieseline H640/630. **Thermal fleece** is perfect for table runners and place mats, oven mitts and lunch boxes as it helps to keep the heat/cold in or out! Bosal makes a good one.

**Foam** can also be fusible or sew-in, I use this for bags and boxes that I need to be quite firm. It's around ¼in (6mm) in thickness but is easy to sew with. I like Bosal In-R-Form Single-Sided Fusible Foam Stabilizer.

For hats, belts, bags and storage boxes where you need a firmer interfacing, choose a non-woven polyester/viscose stabilizer such as Decovil, again available in different thicknesses. I'd only use the heavy version on larger projects as it can be quite tricky if you need to turn it through on projects like lined bags.

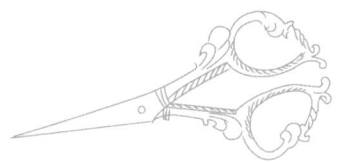

# Fabric care and laundry tips

The last thing you want is to take all that care making or mending your garments only for them to shrink or fray in the wash! Check laundry care labels on your clothes and the fabrics you buy.

## COMMON LAUNDRY SYMBOLS

Wash up to 30°C | Wash up to 40°C | Wash up to 60°C | Hand wash | Do not wash

Professional dry clean only | Do not dry clean | Tumble dry | Do not tumble dry

Iron at low temperature | Iron at medium temperature | Iron at high temperature | Do not iron

## PRE-WASHING FABRIC

To pre-wash or not? Honestly? I don't! Unless I'm dressmaking and the slightest shrinkage may affect the fit of a garment. For items that don't go in the washing machine – bags, curtains, cushion covers – I spot clean instead of washing.

It's your choice when preparing fabrics for quilting; personally I like a bit of shrinkage as it gives a quilt a vintage feel, but if you're not sure, pre-wash anyway!

Avoid washing pre-cut fabrics as they may fray, and you may find your fat quarters and fabric strips are smaller than you thought if washed before sewing.

## My fabrics...

It's a good idea to test out new fabrics before you start your projects. Why not make a few stitches on a swatch to see how it looks and behaves? Record some notes below for future reference.

..................................................................................................
..................................................................................................
..................................................................................................
..................................................................................................
..................................................................................................
..................................................................................................
..................................................................................................
..................................................................................................
..................................................................................................
..................................................................................................
..................................................................................................
..................................................................................................
..................................................................................................
..................................................................................................
..................................................................................................
..................................................................................................
..................................................................................................
..................................................................................................

### Tip

Can't figure out which way up your fabric is? Listen to it! The warp is generally a tighter weave than the weft, and by tugging the fabric sharply in both directions you'll hear a higher pitch in the warp.

## Fabrics that are special to me...

We all have those treasured fabrics – a favourite shirt, blanket or something that brings back precious memories. Write them here and why they are important to you.

Stick a photo of your favourite fabric here, or a swatch if you have one.

# My fabric stash...

*Stick your fabric swatch here.*

Name and brand of fabric: ..................................................

..................................................................................................

Fabric type: ..........................................................................

Colour reference: ................................................................

How much do I have? ........................................................

Where to buy more: ..........................................................

*Stick your fabric swatch here.*

Name and brand of fabric: ..................................................

..................................................................................................

Fabric type: ..........................................................................

Colour reference: ................................................................

How much do I have? ........................................................

Where to buy more: ..........................................................

*Stick your fabric swatch here.*

Name and brand of fabric: ..................................................

..................................................................................................

Fabric type: ..........................................................................

Colour reference: ................................................................

How much do I have? ........................................................

Where to buy more: ..........................................................

*Stick your fabric swatch here.*

Name and brand of fabric:

Fabric type:

Colour reference:

How much do I have?

Where to buy more:

**31 SEWING ESSENTIALS**

*Stick your fabric swatch here.*

Name and brand of fabric:

Fabric type:

Colour reference:

How much do I have?

Where to buy more:

*Stick your fabric swatch here.*

Name and brand of fabric:

Fabric type:

Colour reference:

How much do I have?

Where to buy more:

## SEWING ESSENTIALS

*Stick your fabric swatch here.*

Name and brand of fabric: ..................................................
..................................................
Fabric type: ..................................................
Colour reference: ..................................................
How much do I have? ..................................................
Where to buy more: ..................................................

*Stick your fabric swatch here.*

Name and brand of fabric: ..................................................
..................................................
Fabric type: ..................................................
Colour reference: ..................................................
How much do I have? ..................................................
Where to buy more: ..................................................

*Stick your fabric swatch here.*

Name and brand of fabric: ..................................................
..................................................
Fabric type: ..................................................
Colour reference: ..................................................
How much do I have? ..................................................
Where to buy more: ..................................................

**SEWING ESSENTIALS**

Stick your fabric swatch here.

Name and brand of fabric: ................................................
................................................................................
Fabric type: ....................................................................
Colour reference: ............................................................
How much do I have? ....................................................
Where to buy more: ......................................................

Stick your fabric swatch here.

Name and brand of fabric: ................................................
................................................................................
Fabric type: ....................................................................
Colour reference: ............................................................
How much do I have? ....................................................
Where to buy more: ......................................................

Stick your fabric swatch here.

Name and brand of fabric: ................................................
................................................................................
Fabric type: ....................................................................
Colour reference: ............................................................
How much do I have? ....................................................
Where to buy more: ......................................................

Stick your fabric swatch here.

Name and brand of fabric:

Fabric type:
Colour reference:
How much do I have?
Where to buy more:

Stick your fabric swatch here.

Name and brand of fabric:

Fabric type:
Colour reference:
How much do I have?
Where to buy more:

Stick your fabric swatch here.

Name and brand of fabric:

Fabric type:
Colour reference:
How much do I have?
Where to buy more:

*Stick your fabric swatch here.*

Name and brand of fabric:

Fabric type:

Colour reference:

How much do I have?

Where to buy more:

*Stick your fabric swatch here.*

Name and brand of fabric:

Fabric type:

Colour reference:

How much do I have?

Where to buy more:

*Stick your fabric swatch here.*

Name and brand of fabric:

Fabric type:

Colour reference:

How much do I have?

Where to buy more:

**SEWING ESSENTIALS**

# My fabric wish list...

Keep a note of gorgeous fabrics you've spotted online or on a shopping trip that you'd like to add to your stash. Write down if you're looking for a particular fabric for a project, to remind you if you spot something suitable.

..................................................................................................

..................................................................................................

..................................................................................................

..................................................................................................

..................................................................................................

..................................................................................................

..................................................................................................

..................................................................................................

..................................................................................................

..................................................................................................

..................................................................................................

..................................................................................................

..................................................................................................

..................................................................................................

..................................................................................................

..................................................................................................

## DO I NEED MORE FABRIC?

Do I need more fabric?
I ask myself each day.
My head says no, my heart says yes,
My heart always gets its way.

Do I need more fabric?
Do I have the cash?
Is this quite indulgent
To keep building up my stash?

Do I need more fabric?
I see it, I have to have it!
Is this just good practice
Or a naughty little habit?

Do I need more fabric?
I already have so much...
But I only sew with half of it,
The rest I just like to touch.

Do I need more fabric?
My cupboards couldn't be fuller!
But when I start a project
I just have to have the right colour!

Do I need more fabric?
You don't have to guess
That when I'm asked the question
The answer is always YES!

# Threads

There are so many types of threads it's easy to lose your... thread! So here's a basic guide.

- The larger the number on your thread spool, the narrower the thread, so a 40wt is stronger than a 50wt – these are the two standard medium weights you'll use the most.
- Fine weights range from 60wt to 100wt – good for appliqué or quilting where you want the stitches to blend into the fabric.
- Heavy weights go up to a 3wt, but don't use anything thicker than a 12wt with your sewing machine.
- Threads are either natural or synthetic. Choose cotton thread if you're sewing natural fibres and polyester thread with man-made fabrics and knits. If you're unsure which to use, a cotton-wrapped polyester is a good choice!
- To be honest, if I'm making something like a bag, I go for the colour of thread I like without paying too much attention to the fibre content. Oops... did I say that out loud?
- If you use an overlocker/serger, be sure to use the correct thread. Overlocker threads are finer than sewing machine threads to reduce bulk at the seams, and the machine uses at least three threads to make the seams strong. You could use regular thread in an overlocker but it will take so much you'll be changing spools every few minutes! I have, however, used overlocker thread in the bobbin in my machine with some success...

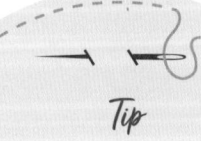

**Tip**

Problems with needle threading? Spray a little hairspray onto your thumb and forefinger and slide the thread through them. This will stiffen the thread to make it easier to pass through the eye of the needle.

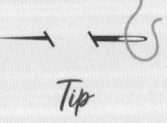

**Tip**

Beeswax helps thread to travel smoothly through fabric when hand sewing. Gently pull the thread through the beeswax to coat it. If you don't have beeswax, try a lip balm – it works a treat!

# Zips

Here are some of the zips I use most frequently.

**Continuous zipping** This is bought in lengths; sometimes the sliders are already attached, sometimes you need to attach them yourself. Extra sliders are usually available.

**Nylon zips** The most common type of zip. I choose a zip that is longer than I need, which means I can sew with the slider out of the way, and it can be cut to size so I don't have to worry about buying the exact length of zip I need.

**Nylon zips with transparent tape** Perfect for lightweight fabric or for a fabric colour that's difficult to match.

**Metal-tooth zips** These are strong zips that are good for outerwear and jeans. They have individual metal teeth that are fixed evenly along the tape.

**Open-ended zips** Metal or plastic teeth are fixed along the zip tape. The two sides of the zip come apart completely, making the zip perfect for coats and jackets.

**Invisible zips** The zip shouldn't be seen when fitted, apart from the teardrop-shaped zip pull.

## TIPS WHEN USING ZIPS

- To help a zip run smoothly, try rubbing lip balm, candle wax, soap or a graphite pencil over the teeth. Wipe off any residue.
- Pin your zip in place, then hand tack/baste and remove the pins before sewing. Alternatively, you may find it easier to use a temporary glue instead of tacking/basting your zip by hand, or a fusible quilter's tape may help. Use whichever method you prefer – the important thing is that it enables you to sew a precise line without manoeuvring around pins, and it helps to keep the zip coil centred.
- When approaching the slider as you're sewing in a zip, leave the needle in the down position and manoeuvre the slider out of the way. This will help to keep your stitch line straight.

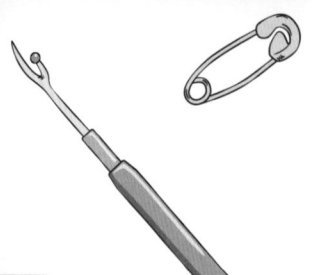

# Your tool kit

## NEEDLES

### MACHINE NEEDLES

I always think of the needle as the 'fuse' in your machine – if the fabric is too thick for the needle, the needle will break, saving damage to your machine! If you see skipped or uneven stitches this may be because you're using the wrong needle for the job. Change it for the right one and try again!

Types of needles:

- **Sewing machine needles** are sized in both metric (sizes 60–110) and imperial (size 8–18). The smaller the number, the finer the needle. The metric numbers depict the diameter of the needle, so an 80/12 will measure 0.8mm across.
- For most of your projects a **universal needle** will be fine. It's worth investing in an assortment of sizes to suit different weights of fabric. For dressmaking I generally use 80/12, for jeans I'd say 90/14 and for quilting I use 90/14.

The needles I also like to keep in my sewing box are:

- **Sharps**, good for densely woven fabrics and layers with wadding.
- **Jeans/denim needles** which have a strong shank for coping with thick fabrics.
- **Ball point/jersey needles** which have a slightly rounded point to prevent knitted fabrics from laddering.
- **Top stitch needles** are strong and have a large eye to take thick thread.

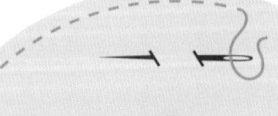

### Tip

Machine needles are often colour coded, but if they're not and you don't recognize them out of their packets, dab a little coloured nail varnish on the shanks – you could use the colours opposite.

- You may also like **twin needles** for pintucking or making decorative borders. You won't be able to use your needle threader or thread-cutting functions on your machine with these needles.
- **Metafil needles** are perfect for metallic and embroidery threads.
- **Quilting needles** are designed to go through multiple layers of fabric for even stitching.
- **Leather needles** have a chisel shape with a pointed end. Just use these with genuine leather and suede, not PU or laminates – keep your jeans needle for those fabrics!

## MACHINE NEEDLE GUIDE

| Fabric type | Needle size | Thread weight |
|---|---|---|
| **Very fine**<br>Fine lace, voile, chiffon, fine silk, organza | 60/8<br>65/9<br>10/10 | 60–80 |
| **Light weight**<br>Synthetics, cotton voile, silk, lycra, spandex, lawn | 75/11<br>80/12 | 50–60 |
| **Medium weight**<br>Cotton, linen, jersey, fleece, fine corduroy, knits, velvet, sweatshirt knits, poplin | 90/14 | 40–60 |
| **Heavy weight**<br>Denim, canvas, leather, suiting, corduroy | 100/16 | 40–50 |
| **Very heavy**<br>Upholstery fabric, heavy denim, heavy canvas, faux fur | 110/18+ | 20–40 |

### Needle types and common colour coding

| | | | |
|---|---|---|---|
| ○ None | Universal | ● Purple | Microtex |
| ● Yellow | Stretch | ● Orange | Jersey |
| ● Red | Universal twin | ● Brown | Leather |
| ● Blue | Jeans | ● Light blue | Ball point |
| ● Green | Quilting | | |

SEWING ESSENTIALS

## HAND SEWING NEEDLES

The bigger the number, the finer and shorter the needle. There are several types of hand sewing needles designed for different purposes.

My favourite go-to for almost everything is a **Sharps number 9**, it's long and slim but with a round eye that I can actually see to thread!

**Millinery needles** are another choice for me – I don't tend to make hats, but I like the longer length of these needles.

**Crewel needles** are good for embroidery, and **darners** for thick threads and wool.

As with your machine needles, keep a selection of different sizes in your sewing kit. I'm sure you'll find your favourite to work with too!

## CUTTING TOOLS

**Scissors/shears**

I'd suggest three pairs of scissors:
- **Dressmaking shears** for fabric cutting.
- **A small pair of snips** for cutting into seams and cutting off threads
- **Paper scissors** for patterns. There are many different types of scissors and shears available, but these are your basic must-haves.

**Rotary cutter**

I use three sizes of rotary cutter:
- 60mm (2⅜in) for large projects such as curtains, or for cutting through thicker fabrics and foam.
- 45mm (1¾in) for most other projects.
- 28mm (1⅛in) for more intricate cutting as with dressmaking patterns.

If you only buy one rotary cutter the 45mm (1¾in) is the most popular choice, and the most useful. Always put on the guard when the cutter is not in use, and never cut towards you, these things are sharp! Also avoid pins on your cutting mat: one pin can ruin a blade.

I mainly cut using a rotary cutter with an acrylic ruler, but for patterns I cut with the rotary cutter freehand. Try it and you may find it easier than cutting with scissors as you won't need to lift the fabric. Well worth practising if you're a bit uncertain!

**Cutting mats**

Buy a mat as large as you have room for! Mats are printed in imperial, metric and sometimes both, and are handy when used with a ruler for not just measuring accurately, but cutting at angles such as on the bias. Use a smaller mat for smaller projects, or if you're short on space.

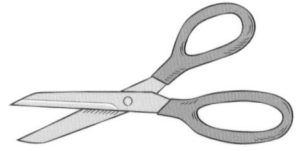

# MEASURING TOOLS

**Tape measure**
Plastic tape measures are more accurate than fabric, but may stretch over time, so replace them every now and then.
   Try gluing a tape measure to the front of your cutting table! This is particularly handy for measuring large widths of fabric.
   Did you know that plastic tape measures are ⅝in (1.5cm) wide? That means you can use the width of the tape to mark seam allowances.

**Rulers**
A yard/metre stick is useful for larger projects like curtains.
   Acrylic rulers are necessary for patchwork. I'd recommend a 24 x 6in (60 x 15cm) ruler to give the cleanest and most accurate cut, particularly for quilting. I also find a 12 x 6in (30 x 15cm) ruler handy for smaller projects.
   Square rulers make cutting triangles a breeze and shaped acrylic templates help with patchwork shapes.

# OTHER TOOLS

**Pins**
There are many pins for many purposes, but for most of my projects, quilting, homewares or dressmaking I use flower head pins – I like the length and large heads that I can see if I drop them! Glass head pins can be ironed over but may leave a dent in the fabric. Fine fabrics can be pinned in the seam allowance so as not to leave holes.

**Marking tools**
My favourites are heat-erasable pens, but beware! They're not designed for fabric and may mark particularly dark fabrics, so are best used within a seam allowance. Air and water-erasable pens work well, but will become permanent if ironed, so avoid using them if you're pressing as you sew. Air-erasable pen will disappear after a few hours so is not to be used on an ongoing project. Chalk comes in many colours and will stand out on darker or patterned fabrics.

**Iron and ironing board**
An iron is essential to iron creases out of tissue paper patterns, iron fabric flat before cutting, and pressing seams, pleats and darts. Always iron a patch test on scrap fabric first to make sure you have the correct heat setting. I prefer a steam-generator iron that has been designed to be left on for extended periods of time, with an automatic shut-off. A travel iron can also be handy for small projects.

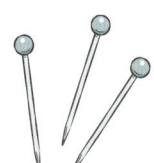

# My tools...

**Tools I have:**

**Brands I like using:**

# My tools wish list...

Tools I'd like to add to my collection:

### Tip
Magnetic knife holders make perfect storage for your tools!

# Sewing machines

## Mechanical vs computerized

Although computerized machines are generally more expensive than mechanical, I do think they are worth the investment.

Mechanical machines are considered more basic, with knobs to adjust the settings. Computerized machines tend to have a wider stitch choice and automatic features such as needle up/down positioning and thread cutting.

If you're just starting on your sewing journey, remember you won't be a beginner for long so buy a machine that has more features than you think you need. Personally I go for a needle threader, needle up/down function and a drop feed dog facility for free-motion sewing. Always choose a big brand machine for the peace of mind of a long warrantee and ongoing support.

Clean your machine on a regular basis (keep a note opposite to remind yourself when you cleaned it last), particularly if you're using fibrous fabrics like fleece. Always read your manual before cleaning, but generally you'll take off the throat plate and remove the bobbin before twiddling a small brush inside to scoop up any lint (reminds me of candy floss!). Remember to dust in between the feed dogs. It's amazing how much better your machine will sew after a good clean! Don't blow into the machine as you'll introduce damp, and all you'll do is push lint further into the machine. Consult the manual to see if and where you need to add oil.

It's recommended you change your needle after around eight hours of sewing. Well, I don't count, but I'll change mine after every three or four projects. You can actually hear a blunt needle as it 'bashes' onto the fabric instead of cutting through!

### Tip

Keep a magnet by your sewing machine to pick up dropped needles and pins that you may not be able to see.

# My sewing machine...

It's handy to write down when and where you bought your sewing machine and keep track of when it's cleaned. Perhaps even jot down where you keep the manual for easy finding!

**My sewing machine notes:**
....................................................................................................
....................................................................................................
....................................................................................................
....................................................................................................
....................................................................................................

Date cleaned: ................................
Notes: ................................

Date cleaned: ................................
Notes: ................................

Date cleaned: ................................
Notes: ................................

Date cleaned: ................................
Notes: ................................

Date cleaned: ................................
Notes: ................................

Date cleaned: ................................
Notes: ................................

Date cleaned: ................................
Notes: ................................

Date cleaned: ................................
Notes: ................................

# Sewing machine stitches

Some machines have just a few basic stitches and some are quite comprehensive, so take a look at your manual to learn more about them. Here are my most-used.

**Straight stitch**
The most common stitch, used for seams, top stitching, basting/tacking and gathering. Use the longest stitch length for tacking, and loosen the top tension slightly for gathering.

**Triple straight stitch**
Two stitches forward then one back. This stitch is useful for stretch fabric and creates a bold line for top stitching.

**Zig zag**
To finish off raw edges, used on stretch fabric and appliqué – this is a really versatile stitch! Shorten the length to create a solid line for appliqué (satin stitch), or use as a decorative stitch to top stitch around pockets, hems and bag flaps. For stretch fabric, reduce the width of the stitch.

**Lightening stitch**
This looks like a zig zag stitch at an angle, and is used for stretch fabrics.

**Button hole stitch**
Some machines will use a four-step button hole, some a one-step. Four-step means you stitch the bottom of the button hole, change the stitch to the left side, then the top, then back down the right side. A one-step has a foot with space at the back to sit the button in so that the machine can gauge the size, then sews in one without stopping until finished.

The most-used shape is rectangular. Round-ended button holes are generally used on blouses, and keyhole button holes are for heavier fabrics or buttons with shanks.

**Overcasting stitch**
This takes the stitch slightly over the raw edge of the fabric to help prevent fraying, and looks similar to an overlocker/serger stitch.

**Blind/invisible hem**
Your machine will probably come with a blind hem foot. Use this as a guide when hemming to create a barely seen stitch on garments or curtains. The stitch is also useful for appliqué where you don't want the stitches to stand out.

**Decorative stitches**
My favourite is simple blanket stitch – my go-to stitch for appliqué or finishing edges, but many machines will have a variety of both pretty and practical stitches. Experiment with stitch lengths and widths, and try embroidery or metallic threads to create special effects!

# My stitch settings...

Always test your stitches first on a spare piece of the fabric you will be using to make sure the length, width and tension is as you want it. Make a note below of your most-used and favourite stitches and settings.

..........................................................................................

..........................................................................................

..........................................................................................

..........................................................................................

..........................................................................................

..........................................................................................

..........................................................................................

..........................................................................................

..........................................................................................

..........................................................................................

..........................................................................................

..........................................................................................

..........................................................................................

..........................................................................................

...........................................................

...........................................................

...........................................................

### Tip

Always read your sewing machine manual! Your machine may have more features than you thought.

# Tension

Oh tension, you poor thing! You always get blamed for wonky stitching! The only time I touch the tension is if I'm using metallic threads or want an effect like shirring or gathering. If you end up with skipped stitches, or 'nests' of thread under your fabric, try the tips below before touching the tension dial.

**Re-thread the machine:** 90 per cent of threading problems can be sorted this way. If thread is knotting under your fabric then it's a top tension issue. Re-thread the machine with the presser foot up until it comes to the needle, then put the foot down. When up, the tensions are disengaged and the thread flows freely. When down, the tensions are engaged and the thread should feel tight. Make sure the thread has a clear passage through the threading system. Check the thread spool itself as sometimes thread can catch on any little nicks on the spool.

**Change your needle:** thread that is too thick or thin for the needle may cause skipped stitches.

**Check the needle:** the needle should be pushed right inside the needle clamp.

**Use the correct size spool cap for your thread spool:** if it's too large, thread may catch on it as you sew, if it's too small, thread may catch on the spool. The cap should ideally be the same size as the spool.

**Clean the spool pin:** black sticky glue from the labels can get stuck on spools and hinder the path of the thread.

**Check the bobbin:** an overfilled or loosely filled bobbin can affect tension – make sure it is well wound. When filling the bobbin make sure you use the tension guide on your machine, to ensure perfect tension in the bobbin thread.

## OTHER PROBLEMS YOU MAY COME ACROSS

**Fabric not feeding:** feel the underside of the presser foot as it may be worn.

**Your stitch length is too short:** thread may be caught.

**Not enough presser foot pressure:** most machines have a dial you can turn to increase this.

**Feed dogs are down:** did you just do some free motion embroidery? Clean the feed dogs.

**Fabric puckering:** change the needle.

**Stabilizer needed:** re-thread the machine, the thread may be caught. Is the needle right for the fabric?

If you have persistent problems, it's a good idea to find a local servicer to take a look at your machine – it may be something only they can fix!

### DON'T BLAME TENSION!

My thread's getting knotty,
Needle jammed with a jolt,
But don't blame the tension...
It's not tension's fault.

I'm looking at a bird's nest!
I've come to a halt!
But please don't blame tension...
It's not tension's fault.

Firstly take out all the thread,
And then re-thread again,
But don't touch the tension,
Tension's not to blame.

Then try a new needle,
Then try some new thread,
But don't touch that tension dial,
That's not the fault, I said!

Try taking off the needle plate
And cleaning out the fluff,
Don't blame the tension,
It could be other stuff.

Now my seams are perfect,
Feel free to take a look!
I didn't blame the tension,
Tension's off the hook!

# Colour

## CHOOSING COLOURS

Choosing colours for a project, particularly when quilting, can be quite overwhelming. There are so many shades of colour, how do you choose which goes with what? Here's where a colour wheel may help.

Arranged around the wheel are the primary colours – red, blue and yellow – and when mixed together they produce secondary colours (think red and yellow make orange). Then the tertiary colours are secondary colours mixed with primary colours, so red and orange produces deep red/orange, and so on. There are many more shades but let's not make this too complicated!

One half of the wheel is warm tones, the other is cool tones. Colours on the wheel that are opposite each other are complementary. So if you're choosing two colours, try blue and yellow, deep orange/red with blue/green and see if you like the combinations.

A group of three colours next to each other are analogous colours. Try blocking out all the other colours with your hands and see how different groups of three work for you.

If you have a particular colour that you'd like to match, for instance you need something to go with a blue/green, match the fabric to the colour wheel then look at the opposite side of the wheel – red/orange makes a perfect contrast! On the other hand if you have a selection of fabrics and you're not sure if they match, place each fabric over its matching colour on the wheel and see how they sit together.

The colour wheel may help with matching colours, but ultimately the choice of colour is whatever makes you happy, no rules apply!

Warm colours tend to stand out more than cool colours, neutrals are good for backgrounds as they don't like centre stage, although white does tend to stand out in a crowd, and black makes a stunning background for vibrant colours.

# Colour combinations

The colour combinations below may not match the colour wheel exactly, but they work! Tonal colours, brights together and pastels together create a pleasing effect, as do shades of the same colour.

# Choosing patterns with colour

Try combining different prints and plain fabrics of the same colour. This strawberry fabric works with a plain or a check, a spot may be too close to the strawberry design to stand out. Choose colours that aren't obvious; with this fabric I'd tend to go for reds, but the print looks different when teamed with the subtle green in the leaves. Explore the colours of your fabric before you make a choice!

Be creative and try stripes in different directions, checks or spots in different colours, but try to keep the scale the same for the best effect.

Many fabric manufacturers will create collections of prints that are designed to work together so you don't need to find suitable matches. Sometimes their choices are quite unexpected but just work!

### Tip

Be aware of pattern placement on large prints; it's not too flattering to have a big flower on your tummy!

# My colours...

**My favourite colours:**

...........................................................................................................................................
...........................................................................................................................................
...........................................................................................................................................
...........................................................................................................................................
...........................................................................................................................................

**Colours that suit me:**

...........................................................................................................................................
...........................................................................................................................................
...........................................................................................................................................
...........................................................................................................................................
...........................................................................................................................................

**Colours that make me happy:**

...........................................................................................................................................
...........................................................................................................................................

**My calming colours:**

...........................................................................................................................................
...........................................................................................................................................

My favourite colour combinations:

Colour themes for the home:

# PROJECT PLANNING

It's time to get organized! It's worth taking the time to prepare your work space and plan your projects. There's nothing worse than getting halfway through a project and not having everything you need!

# Getting organized

Have you ever started a project and not finished it because you didn't have all the components? Or maybe you had the components but just couldn't find them! Or you found the perfect fabric online but couldn't remember where? Use this section of your journal to keep notes on all your current and future sewing projects.

Write lists of projects you are yet to finish (I'm sure we all have those!) and projects you'd like to make on pages 60–61. Use the 20 project planners on pages 62–141 to help you plan out each exciting new project and fill in all the information you can, so you know exactly what you need before you start sewing.

Take a look at the materials and notions you already have, then make a note of what you need and where to buy it from.

You don't need to finish each project in one go, but do make a note of when you started and any issues you come across as you sew.

# Projects to finish...

# Projects to make...

# Project:

**Date started:**

**Date finished:**

**Made for:**

**Sketches:**

**Materials:**

**Notions:**

## Project (continued):

**Machine settings:**

**Needles:**

**Threads:**

**Overall cost:**

**What would I change next time?**

## Notes...

Stick a photo of your finished project here.

## Project:

**Date started:**

**Date finished:**

**Made for:**

**Sketches:**

PROJECT PLANNING

**Materials:**

**Notions:**

## Project (continued):

**Machine settings:**

**Needles:**

**Threads:**

**Overall cost:**

**What would I change next time?**

*Notes...*

Stick a photo of your finished project here.

# Project:

**Date started:**

**Date finished:**

**Made for:**

**Sketches:**

**Materials:**

**Notions:**

PROJECT PLANNING

## Project (continued):

### Machine settings:

### Needles:

### Threads:

### Overall cost:

### What would I change next time?

## Notes...

Stick a photo of your finished project here.

# Project:

**Date started:**

**Made for:**

**Date finished:**

**Sketches:**

**Materials:**

**Notions:**

PROJECT PLANNING

**Project (continued):**

**Machine settings:**

**Needles:**

**Threads:**

**Overall cost:**

**What would I change next time?**

## Notes...

Stick a photo of your finished project here.

# Project:

**Date started:**

**Made for:**

**Date finished:**

**Sketches:**

**Materials:**

**Notions:**

PROJECT PLANNING

## Project (continued):

**Machine settings:**

**Needles:**

**Threads:**

**Overall cost:**

**What would I change next time?**

## Notes...

Stick a photo of your finished project here.

# Project:

**Date started:**

**Made for:**

**Date finished:**

**Sketches:**

**Materials:**

**Notions:**

**Project (continued):**

**Machine settings:**

**Needles:**

**Threads:**

**Overall cost:**

**What would I change next time?**

## Notes...

Stick a photo of your finished project here.

## Project:

**Date started:**

**Date finished:**

**Made for:**

**Sketches:**

**Materials:**

**Notions:**

## Project (continued):

**Machine settings:**

**Needles:**

**Threads:**

**Overall cost:**

**What would I change next time?**

## Notes...

Stick a photo of your finished project here.

# Project:

**Date started:**

**Date finished:**

**Made for:**

**Sketches:**

**Materials:**

**Notions:**

## Project (continued):

**Machine settings:**

**Needles:**

**Threads:**

**Overall cost:**

**What would I change next time?**

# Notes...

Stick a photo of your finished project here.

**Project:**

**Date started:**

**Date finished:**

**Made for:**

**Sketches:**

**Materials:**

**Notions:**

## Project (continued):

**Machine settings:**

**Needles:**

**Threads:**

**Overall cost:**

**What would I change next time?**

## Notes...

Stick a photo of your finished project here.

# Project:

**Date started:**

**Date finished:**

**Made for:**

**Sketches:**

**Materials:**

**Notions:**

PROJECT PLANNING

## Project (continued):

**Machine settings:**

**Needles:**

**Threads:**

**Overall cost:**

**What would I change next time?**

## Notes...

Stick a photo of your finished project here.

# Project:

**Date started:**

**Date finished:**

**Made for:**

**Sketches:**

*Materials:*

*Notions:*

PROJECT PLANNING

## Project (continued):

**Machine settings:**

**Needles:**

**Threads:**

**Overall cost:**

**What would I change next time?**

## Notes...

*Stick a photo of your finished project here.*

## Project:

**Date started:**

**Date finished:**

**Made for:**

**Sketches:**

**Materials:**

**Notions:**

PROJECT PLANNING

## Project (continued):

**Machine settings:**

**Needles:**

**Threads:**

**Overall cost:**

**What would I change next time?**

## Notes...

Stick a photo of your finished project here.

# Project:

**Date started:**

**Made for:**

**Date finished:**

**Sketches:**

## Materials:

## Notions:

PROJECT PLANNING

## Project (continued):

**Machine settings:**

**Needles:**

**Threads:**

**Overall cost:**

**What would I change next time?**

## Notes...

Stick a photo of your finished project here.

## Project:

**Date started:**

**Date finished:**

**Made for:**

**Sketches:**

## Materials:

## Notions:

## Project (continued):

### Machine settings:

### Needles:

### Threads:

### Overall cost:

### What would I change next time?

## Notes...

Stick a photo of your finished project here.

**Project:**

**Date started:**

**Date finished:**

**Made for:**

**Sketches:**

**Materials:**

**Notions:**

## Project (continued):

**Machine settings:**

**Needles:**

**Threads:**

**Overall cost:**

**What would I change next time?**

## Notes...

Stick a photo of your finished project here.

## Project:

**Date started:**

**Date finished:**

**Made for:**

**Sketches:**

__Materials:__

__Notions:__

PROJECT PLANNING

## Project (continued):

**Machine settings:**

**Needles:**

**Threads:**

**Overall cost:**

**What would I change next time?**

## Notes...

Stick a photo of your finished project here.

# Project:

**Date started:**

**Made for:**

**Date finished:**

**Sketches:**

**Materials:**

**Notions:**

PROJECT PLANNING

## Project (continued):

### Machine settings:

### Needles:

### Threads:

### Overall cost:

### What would I change next time?

## Notes...

Stick a photo of your finished project here.

**Project:**

**Date started:**

**Date finished:**

**Made for:**

**Sketches:**

**Materials:**

**Notions:**

PROJECT PLANNING

## Project (continued):

**Machine settings:**

**Needles:**

**Threads:**

**Overall cost:**

**What would I change next time?**

## Notes...

Stick a photo of your finished project here.

**Project:**

**Date started:**

**Date finished:**

**Made for:**

**Sketches:**

**Materials:**

**Notions:**

PROJECT PLANNING

## Project (continued):

**Machine settings:**

**Needles:**

**Threads:**

**Overall cost:**

**What would I change next time?**

## Notes...

Stick a photo of your finished project here.

**Project:**

**Date started:**

**Date finished:**

**Made for:**

**Sketches:**

**Materials:**

**Notions:**

## Project (continued):

**Machine settings:**

**Needles:**

**Threads:**

**Overall cost:**

**What would I change next time?**

## Notes...

Stick a photo of your finished project here.

# Monthly planners

In this section we'll write down important dates. This could be shows and exhibitions, tv shows, fabric and book orders, sewing groups or simply birthdays! If you need to remember when a delivery is due or when a favourite item is back in stock, make a short note in the spaces given. Keep these pages up to date and refer to them regularly to make sure you don't miss special events.

**Tips for keeping organized:**

- Make lists! Write things down so you don't forget deadlines and dates.
- Keep your workspace tidy and you'll always know where your things are!
- De-clutter from time to time. Only keep what you need.
- Set goals. Achievable goals will help you to stay focused.

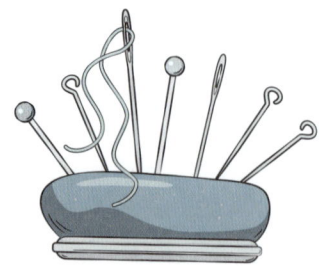

Month:

Year:

Key dates:

Jobs for the month:

PROJECT PLANNING

Month:  Year:

Key dates:

Jobs for the month:

PROJECT PLANNING

Month:  Year:

Key dates:

Jobs for the month:

Month:                              Year:

Key dates:

Jobs for the month:

Month:

Year:

Key dates:

Jobs for the month:

PROJECT PLANNING

Month:

Year:

Key dates:

Jobs for the month:

Month:

Year:

Key dates:

Jobs for the month:

PROJECT PLANNING

Month:                                    Year:

Key dates:




Jobs for the month:

Month:  Year:

Key dates:

Jobs for the month:

Month:

Year:

Key dates:

Jobs for the month:

Month:

Year:

Key dates:

Jobs for the month:

Month:  Year:

Key dates:

Jobs for the month:

# Notes...

# SEWING REFERENCE

In this section we cover some basic sewing terms, words that you may not already know or understand, and abbreviations that can be so confusing! Feel free to scribble your own tips on the pages if there's anything you find that I've missed. We'll also take a look at basic repairs – some things everyone should know whether you can sew or not!

# Mending

One of my mum's sayings was 'don't spend, mend!' And one of the pleasures of being able to sew is that we can do just that, prolonging the life of our garments and saving money at the same time.

## Fabric 'first aid kit'

It's a good idea to always have at least a small sewing kit to hand so you're prepared for any last-minute sewing needs!

- Safety pins are a great temporary mending tool. If a hem comes down or a strap snaps, then simply pin it until you have time to sew.
- However, you can't pin on a button! So a needle and thread is always useful – keep a couple of neutral-coloured buttons in different sizes to hand, just in case you've lost the missing button. A needle or two already threaded with neutral-coloured thread will speed up a repair job.
- A small pair of scissors is handy to snip away unravelling threads – never pull these though or you may end up wearing a little less fabric than you intended!
- A roll of adhesive fabric tape is always handy for a quick fix on hems.
- A small spray bottle of white wine vinegar when applied with bicarbonate of soda works a treat on stains.

## HEMS

So you've caught your heel in your hem and you're not sure how best to fix it? If you're in a hurry then an adhesive fabric tape will work wonders – always have a roll in your 'fabric first aid kit'. Place the tape inside the hem and iron. That's it!

Alternatively re-sew with the invisible hem stitch on your sewing machine, or use a slip stitch by hand.

1. Take your knotted thread inside the folded edge of the hem.
2. Make a stitch of about ¼in (0.5cm) inside the fold then bring the needle out, then into the main fabric, just picking up a few threads.
3. On thicker fabrics you should be able to pick up threads without going all the way through the fabric.
4. Go back into the folded fabric, make a ¼in (0.5cm) stitch and continue until the hem is repaired.

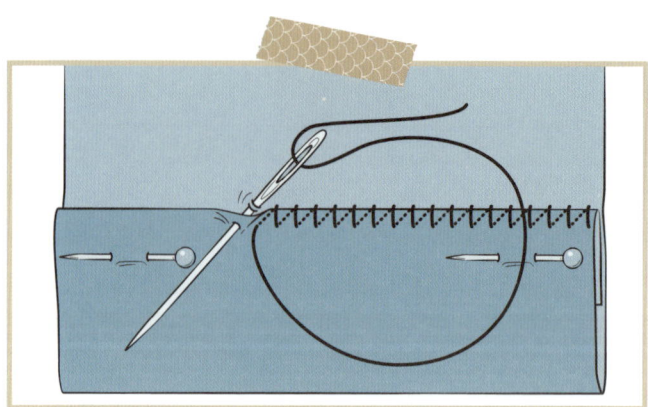

## SPLIT SEAMS

It's happened to us all: you bend, stretch or reach and oops...!

If you can run the split under your machine that's great, but sometimes splits are in places our machine can't easily get to, inside a pocket or the lining in a coat for instance. In these cases a hand-sewn ladder stitch is best.

1. Take a needle and knotted thread through the inside of the seam and out through one side of the split.
2. Take the needle through the opposite side of the split, make a small stitch, then over to the opposite side again. The stitches will look like the rungs of a ladder.
3. Every inch or so, pull the thread to make it tight, and the stitches should blend into the seam. Make the stitches no more than ¼in (0.5cm) in length to sew a strong seam.

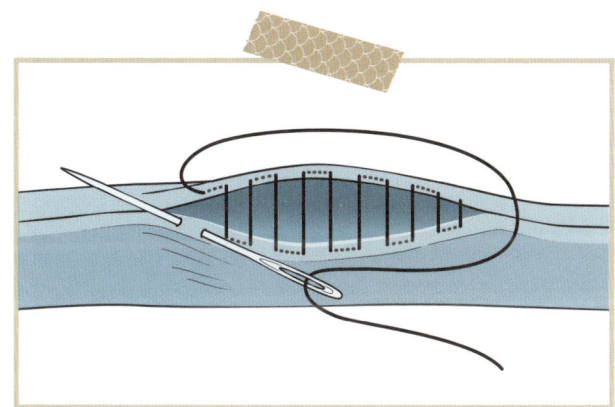

## MENDING HOLES OR SOCKS

When I was younger, we never threw garments away because they had holes in them, we simply mended them, and I think this is an important skill to learn nowadays when we're trying to make everything last a bit longer.

You'll need yarn or thread around the same thickness as the fabric of the garment: yarn if it's knitwear or socks, strong thread for woven fabrics such as jeans (I'd only use this method on small holes). It may be fun to sew the hole in brightly coloured threads to make a feature of the mend!

If you're repairing worn areas of jeans and want the mend to be as invisible as possible, use the darning foot on your sewing machine with blue thread on the top and white on the bottom and sew across the hole in two directions until the hole is covered. It may help to place a woven stabilizer on the back of the repair.

1   Starting at one side, make a long stitch across the hole, then back again.
2   Continue until you have strands of thread covering the hole. Don't pull the stitches tight.
3   Take your needle and weave in and out through the stitches, working perpendicular to the rows you've created, and keeping the new rows as close together as you can – you're creating new fabric!
4   You may find it easier to thread the eye end of the needle through first so you don't catch the threads with the point of the needle.
5   At the end of each row take the needle through the edge of the fabric.

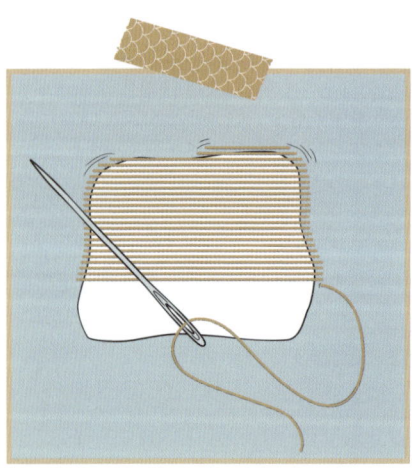
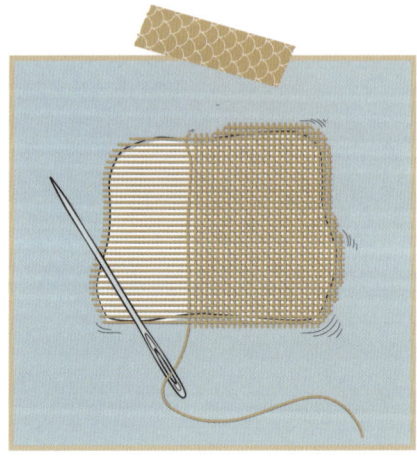

## BUTTONS

If you lose a button from a shirt or cardigan, look at the inside laundry label, you may find a spare! Sometimes there is a spare shirt button at the bottom of the placket. If you have the button that's all well and good!

1. Sew the button back on with strong thread, taking the needle through the holes in the button and through the fabric.
2. Finish by wrapping the thread a couple of times underneath the button, on top of the fabric, so that the button doesn't sit too tightly against the fabric.

If you don't have the button this could be the time to be a little creative – either change all the buttons for new ones, or replace the missing one with a button of a different colour to add a quirky twist!

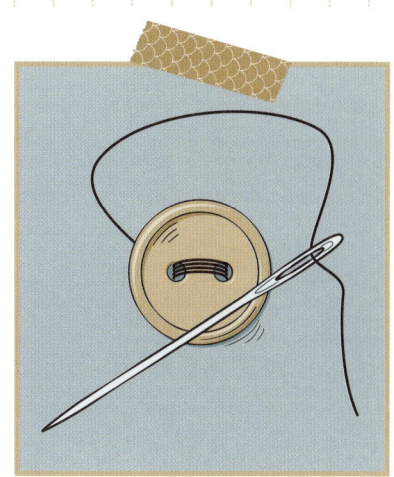

*Tip*

To stop buttons coming loose again, dot a little clear nail varnish over the thread on top of the button.

## PATCHES

A patch over damaged or worn areas of a garment can be quickly turned into a design feature! Brightly coloured fabric behind a hole in a pair of jeans is a fun mend, and sew a few embroidery stitches around the patch to add more interest.

To add a patch from the front:

1. Simply cut a piece of fabric larger than the hole, turn the raw edges over by ¼in (0.5cm) and press.
2. Place the patch over the hole and sew all around.

To add patch from the back:

1. Neaten the hole so that it has straight lines and snip into the corners by ¼in (0.5cm).
2. Fold the edges of the hole inwards by ¼in (0.5cm) and press.
3. Place the patch fabric behind the hole and sew all around.

# Quilting

It is said 'it's not a quilt until it's quilted', and that's so true! Quilting is the method of sewing layers of fabric together – top, backing and wadding in the centre (a 'quilt sandwich') – either by hand or machine. Your first thoughts may be a large quilt to throw on a bed, but you can quilt something as small as an egg cosy!

There are many ways to quilt: by hand, either stitching or tying (which on larger projects may be quite time-consuming but can be relaxing and methodical, and of course a quiet practice as you don't need a machine). If you choose to machine quilt there are so many styles: free motion, in the ditch, echo and using stencils to name a few (see page 164 for more on these). If it's all a little daunting, there's always the professional long arm quilter who will quilt your quilt for you!

A quilt doesn't need to be patchworked. The tops of whole cloth quilts are one piece of fabric, sometimes pre-printed with a design to stitch over. Thread-wise I use a 50–60wt; use a finer thread if you want the stitches to sink more into the work, or heavier to make the stitches bolder. I use the same weight of thread in the top and bottom of my machine.

Quilting needles have a slim point and a strong shaft to cope with multiple layers of fabric, I generally use a 90/14.

I tend to choose 100 per cent cotton fabric for quilting. It works best as it handles beautifully, holds its shape, creases well, is breathable, hard-wearing and available in an endless choice of colours and prints.

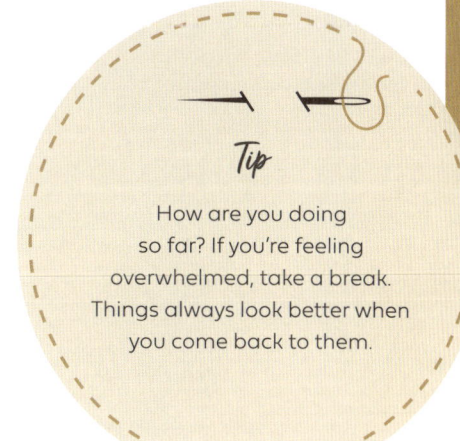

### Tip

How are you doing so far? If you're feeling overwhelmed, take a break. Things always look better when you come back to them.

# Quilting terminology

It's worth getting to know these terms as you'll see them used a lot in project instructions. There are many more but here's a list of my basics…

**Block:** the basic unit of fabric, patchworked, solid or appliquéd, often built up with a repeated pattern.

**Binding:** the fabric strip that finishes the raw edge of the quilt. Bias binding is cut at a 45-degree angle to allow it to be sewn around curves without puckering; binding on straight edges doesn't need to be cut on the bias.

**Border:** the fabric frame that goes around the edge of the quilt.

**Chain piecing:** sewing patchwork pieces together in a continuous line without cutting the thread.

**Echo quilting:** rows of stitches around a shape to 'echo' the design.

**Free motion:** disabling the feed dogs on a sewing machine so that you can move the fabric under the needle in any direction.

**Meandering:** quilting with curved lines that resemble coral, normally free motion stitching.

**Pre-cuts:** bundles of fabric already cut, sold in packs. A great option for quilters, and you will know that the colours and prints in the bundle have been put together to match perfectly. See pages 166–167 for more on pre-cuts.

**Quilt sandwich:** the top and backing of a quilt with wadding/batting 'sandwiched' in the centre.

**Sashing:** strips of fabric that outline each block, making the blocks stand out and also making the quilt larger.

**Single-fold bias binding:** where the edges of the binding fabric are folded to the centre; double fold is where the fabric is folded in half. Double fold is more durable as the edge of the quilt will be covered in two layers of fabric.

**Stitch in the ditch:** stitching over an existing seam; this can help to define the shape of a block without stitching over it.

**Trapunto:** areas of quilting that are stuffed to give them a raised look.

# Quilt sizes

It's always best to measure your bed before making a quilt to fit, but here are some common UK quilt sizes.

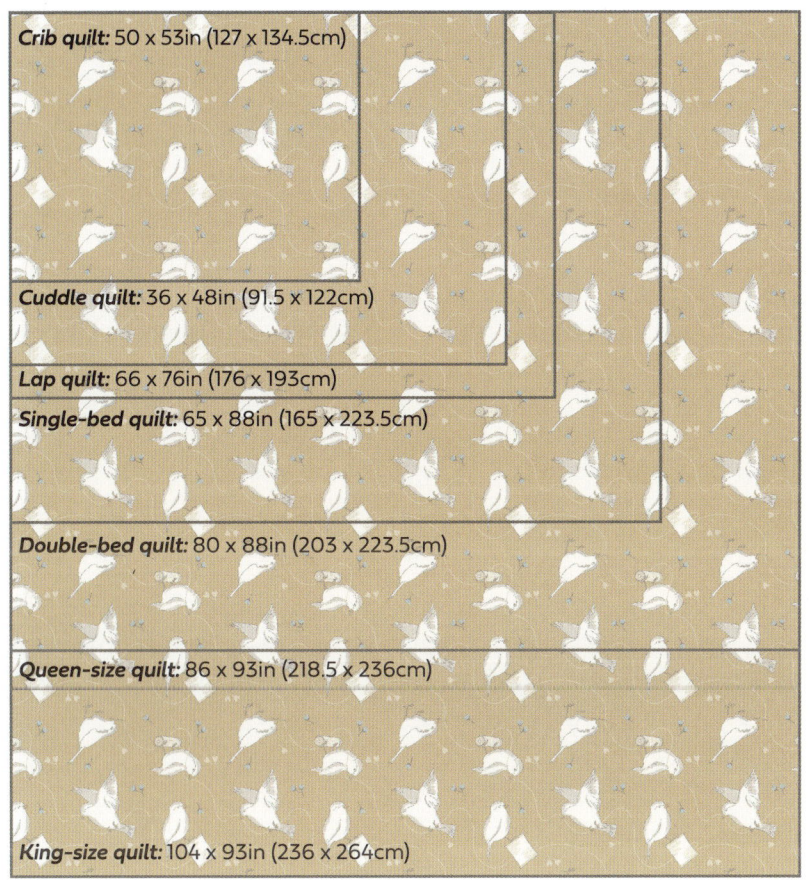

**Crib quilt:** 50 x 53in (127 x 134.5cm)
**Cuddle quilt:** 36 x 48in (91.5 x 122cm)
**Lap quilt:** 66 x 76in (176 x 193cm)
**Single-bed quilt:** 65 x 88in (165 x 223.5cm)
**Double-bed quilt:** 80 x 88in (203 x 223.5cm)
**Queen-size quilt:** 86 x 93in (218.5 x 236cm)
**King-size quilt:** 104 x 93in (236 x 264cm)

# Common fabric pre-cuts

Here are the most common fabric pre-cuts available to buy in the UK. Note that pre-cut sizes can vary in the UK and US, so do double check which one your pattern uses.

**Squares:** packs of square pieces of fabric come in sizes from 1in (2.5cm) to 10in (25cm) and everything in between! Commonly sold in packs are 2½in (6.5cm) and 5in (13cm) squares. These pre-cut squares of perfectly blended colours save you the job of cutting, so you can get on with the fun part – the sewing!

**Strips:** strips of co-ordinating fabrics usually measure 44 x 2½in (112 x 6.5cm) and sometimes come rolled up. These are often sold in packs of 40 strips. The strips can be sewn together or cut into shapes and joined back together again to create patterns.

**Fat quarters:** a yard (metre) of fabric cut into four pieces, each usually measuring 22 x 18in (56 x 46cm).

Each quarter can be cut again (see the chart opposite) and, depending on which way you cut, these pieces will measure either 11 x 18in (28 x 46cm) or 22 x 9in (56 x 23cm). These are fat eighths, which can be cut again to make fat sixteenths.

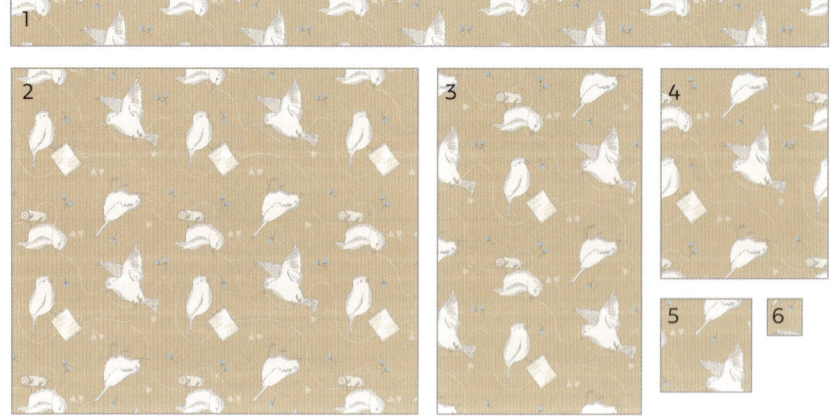

1  Fabric strip: 44 x 2½in (112 x 6.5cm)
2  Fat quarter: 22 x 18in (56 x 46cm)
3  Fat eighth: 11 x 18in (28 x 46cm)
4  Fat sixteenth: 11 x 9in (28 x 23cm)
5  5in square (12.5 x 12.5cm)
6  2in square (5 x 5cm)

# FAT QUARTERS, FAT EIGHTHS AND FAT SIXTEENTHS

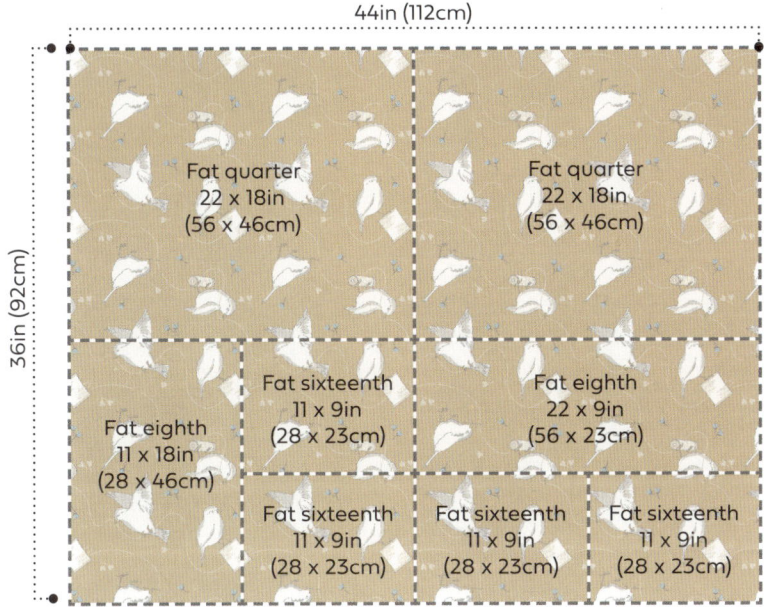

A yard (metre) of fabric.

# Dressmaking

Welcome to a whole world of unique garments made in your choice of fabrics that fit you perfectly! Dressmaking was where I started my sewing journey, albeit for my dolls not myself. I do still have this teddy who is over 60 years old wearing a paisley waistcoat I made when I was about eight years old! The buttonholes were genius… I just cut holes in the fabric – worked for me!

## TOP DRESSMAKING TIPS

- Don't expect your first garment to be couture. You'll learn a lesson each time you sew. Start with a pattern for a garment similar in style and colours to one you already wear, then you'll know it will suit you.
- Plan out the procedure – you have a fabulous journal to do this in after all!
- Try working with jersey – no buttons, zips or darts needed, no finishing seams and the fabric is very forgiving to wear!
- A patterned fabric will disguise wonky stitching better than plain.
- Get your measurements right and make a toile first (see page 171)!
- Try on the garment every step of the way. Small tweaks are easy to make as you sew, rather than waiting until the end and finding the whole thing needs unpicking.
- Hang your garment before hemming. Many fabrics will stretch slightly due to the weight of the garment, so to be sure the hem is straight leave it on a hanger for about 12 hours before hemming.
- Don't be disillusioned if things don't work out first time. Could you drive a car the first time you got into the driving seat, or did you stall a few times? No expert sewer was born an expert! They have all stalled at the start, and the ones that made it just kept on trying.

**WHICH FABRIC TO CHOOSE?**
Poplin, lawn, batik, drill,
Burlap, jersey, crépe, twill,
Most of these I have not met,
Tuille, taffeta, mesh and net...

What do I want or what do I need?
Wool, herringbone, dogstooth or tweed?

That's just the fabric, it gets duller,
Let's talk about the choice of colour...

Forest, pistachio, grass, chartreuse,
I know they're all green,
But which one to choose?

Cerise, fuchsia, salmon pink,
Rose, magenta, I just can't think!

I'll keep it simple,
I'll be alright,
I'll just use cotton,
And only in white!

# Choosing dressmaking patterns

Your pattern is a starting point and can be adapted for perfect sizing. Dress patterns are generally designed for a B cup and generally we're not! Some adjustments may be necessary. For dresses, buy a pattern to fit the bust, it's easier to adjust the hips if needed. The difference between the high bust and full bust determines your cup size: if the difference is more than 2in (5cm) choose a pattern by the high bust measurement. You may still need to adjust the bust, but you'll find that the shoulders fit better.

Most patterns cover several sizes, so if you find you're one size on the top and a different size on the bottom, you can cut across the sizes. If you are in between sizes, choose the larger size.

You'll see a 'finished garment' size that is slightly larger than your body size, this is to allow for 'ease'. If the garment was the same size as you it would be a tight fit and you'd find it difficult to move!

Do a little research from books and videos on how to adjust patterns. There's not enough room in this journal to cover everything!

- Read the information on the back of your pattern before buying fabric. This will tell you the type and amount of fabric needed, plus any notions such as zips and fasteners required.
- Make sure to buy the fabric recommendation on your pattern – the designer knows which fabric type will work best!
- Read and then re-read your pattern before you start cutting or sewing, so you know exactly what to do when you begin.

### Tip

Want to make your tissue patterns last longer? Iron freezer paper on to the wrong sides to make them more durable.

# Dressmaking terminology

**Cut on fold**  Fold the fabric in half, right sides together, and align the edge of the pattern to the fold.

**Negative ease**  This is used with knitted fabrics where the garment is smaller than your body measurements, for a tight-fitting look. (Not for me since the 1970s!)

**Facing**  Usually made from the main fabric, facing is like a partial lining, used to add structure around armholes and necklines.

**Right/wrong side**  The right side of the fabric is the side that you will see on the finished item. On printed fabric the right side is usually brighter in colour, however on woven fabrics you may prefer the opposite, 'wrong' side! If you have a plain fabric and the right and wrong sides look the same, try to use the same side for each pattern piece, as there might be a slight difference you can't see until the project is finished. Take a look under 'Finding and using the selvedge' (page 172) for tips on this.

**Nap**  Fabrics like velvet and corduroy have a short pile which can look shiny in one direction and matt in the other. When cutting out pattern pieces, make sure they all face the same way – if you find one piece is upside down the colour can look very different to the rest. Garments with a nap usually have the nap facing downwards, so that the fabric feels smooth when stroked from top to bottom.

**Notions**  These are your buttons, zips, hook and eyes – basically the closures and accessories your need to make your garment or bag.

**Pressing vs ironing**  Pressing is placing the iron over the seam, whereas ironing involves moving the iron over the fabric, usually without steam. Pressing a seam open therefore doesn't involve any movement of the iron which could distort the fabric. When your project is finished, iron and steam away!

**Raw edge**  The unfinished, cut edge of the fabric.

**Seam allowance**  The distance between the edge of the fabric and the seam line.

**Toile**  A test garment usually made from muslin/calico to make sure the garment fits before cutting into your best fabric.

# More on dressmaking fabric

## FINDING AND USING THE SELVEDGE
The selvedge is the tightly woven edge of the fabric that runs along each side. There may be information on the selvedge you find useful, such as the colours incorporated in the print, or the manufacturer's name.

The selvedge has small holes where the fabric has been attached to tenterhooks when dyed (that's where the phrase 'on tenterhooks' comes from!). These holes can tell you which is the right and wrong side of the fabric – if you run your finger over the holes, one side is smooth and one slightly spiky. The hooks go through the fabric from the back to the front, so the spiky side is the right side. Cut off the selvedges before starting your project.

## TACKING/BASTING
This can be done either by hand or using a long stitch on your machine, and is a temporary stitch that holds layers of fabric together before the final sewing.

## BINDING
A strip of folded fabric that is bound around the edge of a quilt, seam or garment. Bias binding must be used on curves; this is cut at a 45-degree angle to allow the fabric to stretch.

## GRAIN
The directions of the woven threads going either horizontally or vertically in a fabric. The straight grain runs parallel to the selvedge, the cross grain runs between the selvedges.

## WARP AND WEFT
The warp thread runs up and down the fabric, while the weft threads run across from side to side.

### Tip
Can't remember which is the warp and which is the weft? Think 'weft to right'.

## EASE STITCHING
A long stitch that brings fabric fibres together to fit a longer edge to a shorter one, but without gathering the fabric. Used mainly for inset sleeves.

## UNDER STITCHING
For pockets and necklines, this is a way of sewing the seam allowance to the facing to prevent it from rolling out.

## STAY STITCHING
A straight stitch used around curved cuts of fabric to stop them from stretching when sewing.

## CASING
A channel through which to thread elastic or ribbon.

## EASE
The difference between the size of a garment and actual body measurement. If no ease was included in a dress pattern, for instance, the garment would be skintight and difficult to move in. If you're using stretch fabric and want it to be skin-tight, no ease is fine.

## PATTERN MATCHING
If you're nervous about pattern matching then choose a small print or plain fabric that doesn't need matching. Note that checks and stripes can make a garment look twisted if the patterns are not matched at the seams. A large print on curtains that isn't pattern matched can make the curtains look awkward and unprofessional, so always allow extra fabric to accommodate this.

On garments, match the areas that are seen first – front seams and the top of the arms. It's impossible to match every check or stripe so match the most obvious.

For a garment with sleeves, place the front paper pattern piece over the fabric and mark the position of the stripe or check, transfer these markings to the top of the sleeves, then match again to the fabric.

For curtains, fold the long edge of one piece of fabric over by ½in (1.5cm) and press. Place over the second piece of fabric and line up the print. Pin all along the creased line and sew.

The bigger the repeat of the print the more fabric you'll need to allow for matching!

# How to take body measurements

Dressmaking patterns will probably need adjusting to make the perfect fit for your body, so accurate measurements are important. Size is just a number in this case; your dress size in ready-to-wear garments won't necessarily be the same as the dress size on your pattern, so always go by the measurements.

Measure yourself wearing underwear, and snug-fitting or lightweight clothing so you're not adding any extra bulk. Stand in front of a mirror so that you can see that the tape measure is in the correct position.

**High bust** Wrap the tape measure around your chest just under your armpits. Make sure the tape measure isn't twisted, and don't pull too tight.

**Full bust** This is around the fullest part of the bust, usually at nipple height. For men, measure around the widest part of the chest, just under the armpit.

**Waist** To find your waist, take a length of elastic and tie where you find comfortable. Measure around here, leaving the elastic in place as it helps when we get to your centre back and skirt lengths.

**Hips** Measure around the widest part, usually around 8in (20.5cm) down from the waist. Again, make sure the tape measure is straight around the body.

**Back** Measure from the nape of your neck, from the protruding vertebra to the waist. You may need help with this one!

**Dress length** Measure from the nape of your neck to the length you'd like.

**Skirt length** Measure from the elastic around your waist down your side, to the length you need.

**Upper arm** Measure at the fullest part, with your hand on your waist so that your elbow is at a right angle.

**Sleeve length** This is from your shoulder to wrist. Bend your arm slightly and measure along the outside of your arm.

**Inside leg** Place the tape measure as high as you can on your inner thigh and measure to the floor.

**Neck** Measure just above the collar bone all the way around.

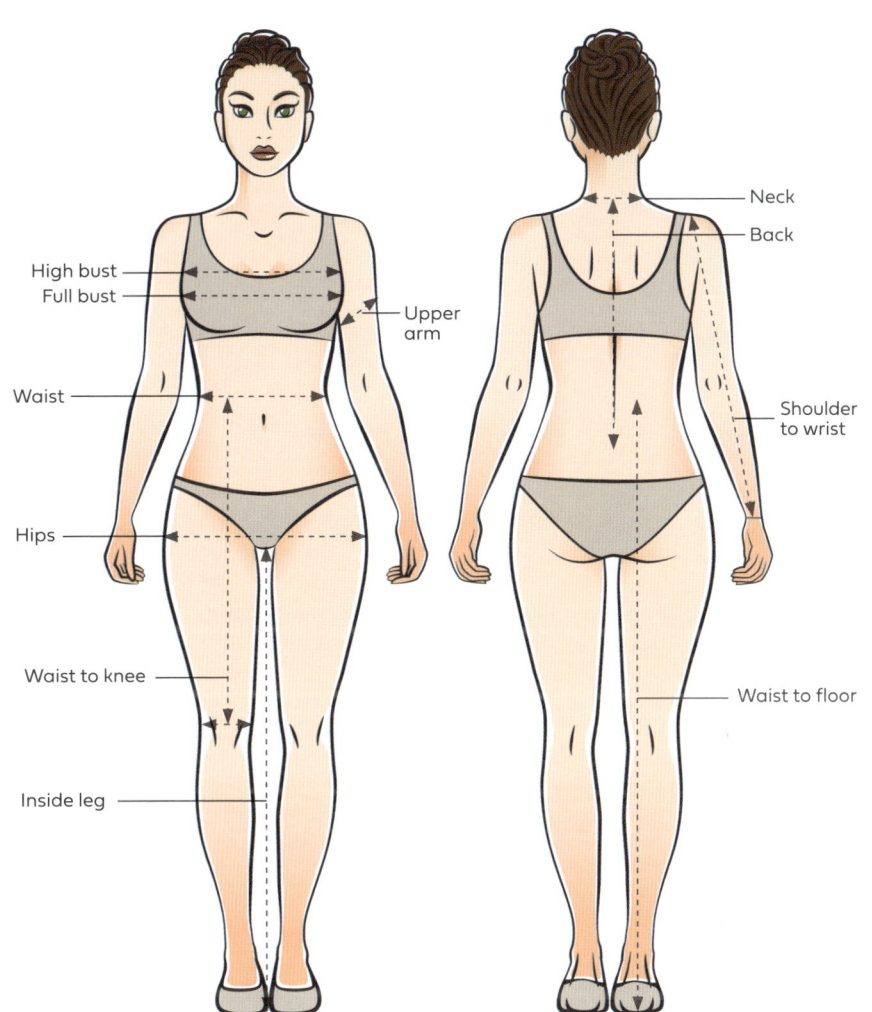

# Homewares

For me, the most satisfying thing about being able to sew is creating something unique, to my exact taste and on a budget. Window dressings, cushions and home décor items can be so expensive to buy, particularly if made to measure, and it is so rewarding to create these things yourself! Think about it – curtains, blinds, cushion covers, throws… they're all rectangles of fabric! The most challenging thing is the cutting, so make sure you have a large, clear area to help keep your fabric flat while cutting. It's an old saying but true: 'measure twice, cut once'… In fact I'd measure three times. If you cut wrongly into a large piece of fabric, it could be costly!

MEASURE TWICE, CUT ONCE!

# Window dressings

Making your own curtains and blinds can be a cost-effective way of dressing your windows. Here's a few tips if you've never made them before.

## CURTAINS

Decide on the look you want – curtains longer than your window can make a room look larger, but avoid covering radiators under the window.

Measure, twice! Measure the length you need then add extra length for the header and hem: I like to use a deep hem of about 5in (13cm) on heavy fabrics, but on fine fabrics only about 2in (5cm). The width of the curtains depends on the type of header you're using, but in general each curtain should be 1.5–2 times the width of the track/pole to give fullness when closed.

When deciding on your fabric bear in mind the pattern repeat: large prints will look better with the pattern matched, so you'll need to buy extra fabric; small prints or plain fabrics won't need pattern matching. I'd also add around 7in (18cm) to the overall width of the fabric for the side seams: the outer fabric needs to be wider than the lining so that it can be folded towards the back of the curtain on each side. A good fabric store should be able to help with fabric requirements if you find you're struggling.

Allow a large area for cutting fabric. This may be the floor – always interesting if you have playful pets!

## BLINDS

There are so many designs – roller, Roman, tied, some are purely decorative and some practical. Measuring is particularly important if your blind is in a recess as it needs to fit the window perfectly. If it is to fit on the outside of the recess, this can be a bit more forgiving!

If the blind is for dressing, maybe behind curtains, a soft or fine fabric may work well. For a more structured, working blind I'd choose heavier fabric which will fold and roll better than fine fabric. Lining with blackout fabric will keep the light out when the blind is down, this also prevents sun damage to your blind fabric.

Look around for kits, they make hanging so much easier!

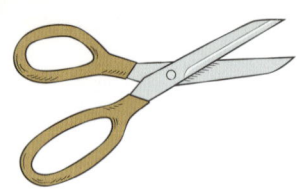

# Bags

Bags are one of my favourite things to sew – and so useful! You can really get creative with patterns and colours, shapes and sizes… And you can never have too many bags!

One of the most important things to take into account is the structure of the bag – do you want it soft or sturdy, big or small? Is it an everyday bag or for special occasions?

- For an everyday bag choose a heavy fabric such as canvas, denim or vinyl, with an interfacing to give it shape. I like fusible foam for a large bag, or fleece if I want a softer, floppier look.
- Use a strong thread, 30–40wt for heavy fabric, and a denim or jeans needle to cope with thick fabrics and layers. Your seams need to be strong for an everyday bag that may carry heavy items.
- Pay attention to the area where the strap is sewn to the bag. Sew in a box shape if the strap is sewn on the outside, or if it's in a seam, sew over the join a few times. Lining also helps a bag keep its shape and strengthen it.
- Use clips instead of pins for thicker fabrics, or for vinyl that may be damaged by pins.
- Reinforce magnetic snaps by adding an extra piece of fabric to the wrong side.
- Add a flap over a zipped pocket to make it even more secure.
- Use a tailor's ham when pressing to keep the shape of the bag from flattening.
- Evening or cosmetic bags can be made with finer fabrics.
- To interface smaller bags, use either fleece or woven interfacing. I really think any bag would benefit from some kind of interfacing, just the fabric on its own would make it very flimsy! If your fabric has a loose weave then use a sew-in interfacing so that the glue doesn't come though the weave. You can always use a basting spray on the fabric side to hold it in place while you sew. You can also use very fluid fabrics such as viscose, or stretch fabrics like jersey, if you use fusible interfacing on the wrong side to stop them stretching!
- Search for the right hardware – it gives your bag a professional finish. Unusual and unique hardware is often found on vintage or preloved shop-bought bags, so check out your local second-hand stores!

# Pillows

Nothing looks more inviting on a sofa or bed than a pile of comfy pillows, and it's a great way of affordably adding colour and style to your décor. Apart from this, they are one of the easiest things to sew!

If you have a neutral room, try adding pillows and accessories in bold colours or even black to really make a statement. If you're wary of large prints and bright colours then cushions are ideal to add a splash without taking over the room!

Contrasting textures create an interesting and modern look – velvet, satin, faux fur, canvas – as long as the colours work together (remember your colour wheel!). Also try different shapes of cushions together – round, square and rectangular, with a bolster thrown in for effect!

For a richer look try finishing your cushions with piping, trims or ruffles, and cushions with text are fun. I used to have one saying 'Dogs not allowed on the sofa'. It didn't work, she can't read...

# Throws/quilts

A quilt to match your décor makes a beautiful accessory thrown over the back of a sofa, chair or bed, and of course is purposeful in chillier weather. But if you're not the quilter, two rectangles of fabric sewn together will work just as well as a useful throw

What's your favourite colour? Make your colour scheme work around shades that you love to make your room a happy place. Choose fabrics that are cosy and drape well, such as fleece and flannels.

*If you have pets like my Bobbin, they'll just love to snuggle up with you on your cosy quilt!*

# Sewing glossary

**Appliqué**
A method of applying a fabric on top of another to create a decorative effect.

**Reverse appliqué**
Where the fabric is applied behind a cut-out shape instead of on top.

**Feed dogs**
These are the 'teeth' under the needle of the sewing machine that pull the fabric through the machine.

**Drop the feed dogs**
A term to describe the lowering of the 'teeth' to prevent the fabric from moving, used in free-motion sewing.

**Free-motion sewing/embroidery**
Using your hands to move the fabric under the needle in a direction or at a speed of your choice. Also used for darning. Drop the feed dogs, or cover them with a darning plate if you don't have the drop facility (in which case your machine will probably have come with a darning plate).

**Fussy cut**
Cutting around a printed motif on your fabric, for instance if you want a flower on the centre of a bag flap, you would place the flap pattern over the flower centrally to position it.

**Pinking shears**
Scissors that cut with a zig zag edge, to help to prevent fraying or to create a decorative effect.

**Quick unpick**
A small, pointed tool that slips under unwanted stitches and cuts through them. Be aware these tools may blunt over time, so always have a few spares.

**Satin stitch**
A short length of zig zag stitch that creates a solid line, used in appliqué. Always practice on a scrap piece of fabric first to make sure you are happy with the look.

**Shirring**
An elastic cord used in the bobbin on your machine, which creates a gathered, stretchy look on garments. Typically used on sun dresses and cuffs.

**Finger press**
Pressing a seam using the pressure of your fingers instead of an iron. Used for smaller projects such as patchwork.

**Grading**
Trimming a seam allowance to reduce bulk.

# Abbreviations

One of the most confusing things about following instructions and patterns is the jargon, terminology and abbreviations. So before reaching for the dictionary, here are a few of the most commonly used abbreviations, and a space for you to note down any new ones you find.

| | | | |
|---|---|---|---|
| **RS** | Right side | **SA** | Seam allowance |
| **WS** | Wrong side | **GL** | Grainline |
| **WOF** | Width of fabric | **RSU** | Right side up |
| **FQ** | Fat quarter | **FMQ** | Free-motion quilting |
| **UFO** | Unfinished object | **HST** | Half square triangle |
| **WIP** | Work in progress | **PP** | Paper piecing |
| **RST** | Right sides together | **EPP** | English paper piecing |
| **WST** | Wrong sides together | **FBA** | Full bust adjustment |
| **RTW** | Ready to wear | **SBA** | Small bust adjustment |
| **CB** | Centre back | | |

Here are a few others of my own...!

| | |
|---|---|
| **TFT** | Time for tea |
| **TFW** | Time for wine |
| **DFTTG** | Don't forget the turning gap |
| **SOTI** | Switch off the iron |

..................................................................................
..................................................................................
..................................................................................
..................................................................................
..................................................................................
..................................................................................

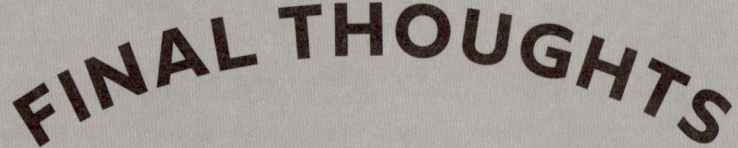

# FINAL THOUGHTS

Ask any sewer why they sew, I bet they'll say one of these things:

*I like to be creative and express myself.*
*It takes my mind off things.*
*I can save money on repairs and shop-bought items.*
*I like to wear unique garments.*

But they'll all say 'because I enjoy it'. Sewing isn't a chore, and most of us don't have deadlines to meet, so relax, take your time and soak up the experience. If things don't turn out well the first time, who's to know? Try again until you're happy. And happy doesn't mean until you've created something perfect – that rarely happens! Be proud of what you've achieved, just look back through this journal and see how far you've come!

## Notes to my future self...

## Things I've accomplished...

New techniques I've tried...

New stitches I've learned...

My favourite project...

I'm proud of myself for...

## SEW-JO

Oh no! Where did it go?
I feel so low,
I just don't know
What on earth happened to my Sew-Jo!

My light isn't lit,
I'm just not fit,
I think I'll quit.
Maybe I'll knit!

I look high and low, ideas there are none.
Has my Sew-Jo gone into room 101?

I took a look
Inside a book.
I was in the mood
For a bit of YouTube.
I paid a sub
To the Half Yard Club.
I made a date
With my Facebook mates.

And don't you know it,
I think I can sew it!
I'm alright Jack,
My Sew-Jo is back!

# Notes...

## Notes...

# Notes...

# Join me in my sewing room!

I was so proud when my first book came out back in 2011. Then *Half Yard Heaven* appeared, selling over 100,000 copies, and since then I have been lucky enough to have written over 30 best-selling books published by Search Press, with more in the pipeline!

I've always wanted to feel close to my readers and to be able to help them on their sewing journey. In 2018 the lovely people at Search Press and I were discussing how I could inspire a new audience of sewers – that was the birth of the Half Yard Sewing Club. Five years later, the Club is bigger and better than ever. I've reached hundreds of thousands of dedicated sewers around the world on social media every year, many of whom have become members.

Joining the Club makes you part of our global sewing community, with exclusive monthly projects complete with downloadable patterns and helpful video instructions. You'll be able to print patterns out at home and start sewing them straight away! As well as monthly projects, you'll get access to the brilliant Half Yard project archive and a library of tips and techniques you can use at any time on your sewing journey. With exclusive offers, giveaways and discounts on books and materials, you'll soon recoup your subscription cost! What's more, you'll be able to join me on the members' forum and my free Facebook Lives and YouTube channels to ask me any questions you might have!

Club favourites, Maddie and Robyn the rag dolls.

What do people love about the Club? Our wonderful member Reinette puts it better than I can when she says, 'the Half Yard Sewing Club offers so much more than just sewing tips and tutorials. We're all one happy family. And the price – it's absolutely value for money.' The Half Yard Sewing Club has brought together an amazing group of people from around the world, in a supportive and creative community where we share, learn from and teach each other, and have fun while we do it!

If you aren't a member yet, you can **try the club for free** with full access to all of my projects. I'm sure you'll love it and you are guaranteed a warm welcome from me and the other members!
Just visit **www.halfyardsewingclub.com/trial** for the details.

See you soon!

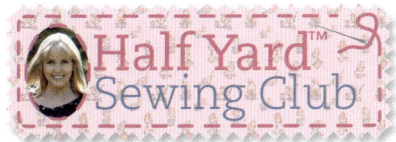

# www.halfyardsewingclub.com

When I think back to my childhood I remember sewing always being a huge part of it. My mum was a seamstress and had a sewing room with cupboards bursting with wonderful fabrics, old biscuit tins full of buttons and threads, and drawers crammed with ribbons and lace. I learnt the love of sewing and creativity from her, and I'm so delighted that my own daughter, Kimberley, is following in both our footsteps.

*Debbie*